Sam

This book belongs to

Leonie

Written by Stephen Barnett
Illustrated by Rosie Brooks

Contents

About this book

This story encourages the new reader to explore the surroundings and to differentiate between characters. The new readers also get to learn new words as they read the story. The questions asked at the end of the book will help readers to revise the words they have read.

Sam the cat

John

Ann

The cat

The cat is Sam.

John
and
Ann

Sam
and
Ann

Here is the cat.

Here is John and here is Ann.

Sam
has a ball.

Sam runs.

Ann runs and John runs.

Where is Sam?

Sam is on the tree.

Ann and John
see Sam.

New words

a	John
and	run
Ann	Sam
ball	see
cat	the
has	there
here	tree
is	where

What did you learn?

What is the colour of the cat?

What is the name of the cat?

How many kids are there?

What is the colour of the ball?